THE SIGHT OF A GOOSE GOING BAREFOOT

THE SIGHT
OF A GOOSE
GOING BAREFOOT

U. S. DHUGA

EYEWEAR PUBLISHING

First published in 2017
by Eyewear Publishing Ltd
Suite 333, 19-21 Crawford Street
Marylebone, London W1H 1PJ
United Kingdom

Cover design and typeset by Edwin Smet
Author photograph by Michael Fraser
Printed in England by TJ International Ltd, Padstow, Cornwall

ISBN 978-1-911335-37-5

Eyewear wishes to thank Jonathan Wonham for his
generous patronage of our press.

WWW.EYEWEARPUBLISHING.COM

U.S. Dhuga's
Harvard Center for Hellenic Studies
monograph *Choral Identity and the Chorus
of Elders in Greek Tragedy* was published
in 2011. His classical music criticism, opera
criticism, and poems have appeared in
*The New Yorker, The Hudson Review, The
New Criterion, PN Review*, and elsewhere.
Founder, Publisher, and Managing Editor
of *The Battersea Review*, Dhuga is a
Classical Philologist and freelance
writer based in Toronto. This is his
debut collection of poetry.

TABLE OF CONTENTS

NOTHING TO BE DONE

Hearing that A-flat was out of tune,
       I exposed the strings of my piano
After practicing this afternoon.
There was nothing to be done about it:
       I called the tuner. But first behind the bow
I found a hair – yours, honey-brown, the ends split.

I wrapped that hair in tissue paper,
       Saved it between two sheets, one marked *largo*,
       One *allegro*: these days are scored just so.
Don't tell me that it's over.
                I know.

AN ACHAEAN SUITOR

for L.E.M.

> So Odysseus strung the great bow without effort.
> Taking it in his right hand, he tested the string:
> And it sounded beautiful, like a swallow's voice.

> – Homer, *Odyssey* 21.409-11

From the time we'd made a habit of sitting
For hours drinking over-steeped tea,
I knew the "us" that had supplanted "me"
Would one day fail: I saw it in the knitting
Of your brow whenever I reached for your hand
And you pulled back. But you always came back
When your single nerve of disbelief went slack,
That nerve whose tautness I could never stand

Nor, in the end, withstand. You played Odysseus,
Stringing with ease the bow whose tautness
Put my strength to shame. The arrogant
Suitor, I went back to feast, ignorant
That you would ever aim an arrow
At my neck, and pluck the bow.

W8 7NL

1.
When I drew my hip-flask from my suit-jacket,
out fell a slip of paper,
folded into fourths, half-torn up the centre
crease – a fragmentary cigarette packet
palimpsest with your ancient blue phone number
whiskey-stained and whiskey-stuck to the pewter
flask. The obverse, as if I never knew,
screamed CIGARETTES CAN KILL YOU.

2.
Perched on a bench in Wandsworth scratching
postcards purchased not for sending,
inside the ticket-pocket of my topcoat
I found the pouch of lavender she'd hoped
would bring me hope. I can smell it still,
the browning purple spilling almost stale
from careless stitches stitched without
a care for lasting. I've bought a ticket
to the Cotswolds. I'm leaving you,
Tooting Bec, for the thatcher's art in Great Tew.

BUTLER LIBRARY

for Prashant Keshavmurthy

Now I see smokestacks
Now Toronto is in plain view
I think back on the Butler Stacks.
Prashant, how did I never know you?

You speculated at Butler Library
On what manner of man I might be.
Here I am. Unshaved, unsuited, no pocket
Square. You hit the ripcord. I hit the net.

MERCURY RETROGRADE

" . . . it is a brutish suffering that 'I' puts up with, sublime
and devastated, for 'I' deposits it to the father's account
[*verse au père – père-version*] . . . "
– Julia Kristeva, *Powers of Horror: An Essay on Abjection*

The rabies came again in my village.
It'll leave February twenty-eight,
Babaji said. I put my dog in his crate
but at night he gnashed his way out, pillaged

the neighbour's goat fodder. So Babaji shot
my dog in the head. I buried him behind
the abandoned *dhaba*: no one would find
him in that disused-lorry-littered lot.

Next morning when I visited the grave
gravel was strewn about; I smelled fresh fumes.
Bhatra Elders, Babaji claimed, consume
myelitic meat when Mercury retrogrades

to reverse their eyes' parallax ellipses.
Babaji shot the Elders. CAUSE: SYNAPSES
RETROGRADE: POST-EXPOSURE PROPHYLAXIS
wrote the coroner. My village has rabies.

THE RISE AND FALL OF
THE PIGOU SOCIETY

My Dear Dhuga,
It is with regret that I write to inform
you of your son's resistance toward Reformed
Epistemology. Apparently
his primary care for the C of E

is that of an aesthete. To provide you but
one example, he has admirably memorised
The Hymnal yet has – his word – 'revised'
The BCP with an 'appendix' entitled 'Jatt
Hypocrisy'. Now I know you are not
of the same faith, but South Asian politics
have no place in the classroom despite his mixed
parentage. He double-dimples the knot

of his Pigou tie and has turned his boater
into a boat. He is one of our brighter
boys but enjoys too much being a nuisance.
I do hope he enjoys Aix-en-Provence

this holiday, but he must remember one
thing: it is a holiday, not a vacation.

Yours sincerely, Mark Morford

SHOALS, ANGLESEY

The shoals that night – I skidded off them, jammed
my thumb against the slick stone, slipped
barefoot: you, in sundered espadrilles, tripped
and stumbled for the crag's recess but slammed

your knee-cap on a plank of refuse garboard.
Afraid that mum would catch us there, we slipped
into the crag, and I (remember?) ripped
the left cuff off my khaki shorts, leaned toward

your knee-cap, wrapped tight your wound, with rhetoric
against you that you, our Neoptolemus,
must steel yourself to save us;
rhetoric against myself that each *tick*

of my watch brought dawn and "*caught!*" quicker on us.
I lied. We will not catch a single clam
tonight. This the first of broken promises
I swear I'll fix, some day . . . that vase, that doorjamb . . .

SELF-PORTRAIT WITH ADORNO

for Robert Archambeau

Ambidextrous. Green.
But Right on matters of spleen.
Cross my median.

LIPSTICK

A dollop of olive oil in the pan,
heat to medium or so – 'not sputter
but sizzle', you'd say. I leave the kitchen

to wash your lipstick off my white linen
shirt. In a pocket somewhere, your number
is in the same lipstick. I wonder, when

you're punishing the Rioja, where are
the husband and kids? Do they awaken
when you stumble on the final stair?

BROLLY

Terrified of such phantoms past and future
as Trust and Safety, we stitched some sutures,

all-purpose, for the phantoms, gave it the name
"Brolly". Brolly withstands winds with a Fox-Frame,

repels the damp and, as topical, too much
sunshine too. Brolly is cotton – but as such

it's finished with a special coat to resist
mould and mildew. So long as Brolly persists,

I thought I'd decorate the all-purpose
umbrage with engraved gold collars: suppose

one of us should lose Brolly altogether –
how might one of us distinguish whether

and which pasts belonged to me, to you, to us
together? I clutch Brolly on the bus

crosstown to the ballet and I receive
so many compliments. The leather sleeve

is so handsome! The contrast stitch is dashing!
Only when I miss my connection, dashing

to the platform of Saint George, does it occur
to me that if we lose Brolly, the blur

of universal catchall might obscure
which defences are phantoms, which are pure.

Nothing can stop me with the gilt tip though,
and the *tap-tap-tap* it sounds in so

many Junction alleyways. One day the rains
will abate, surely, and we'll jam the pains

and cramps and blasted 'things' between Brolly's
ribs and tube, fasten tight the cross-stitch sleeve's

gold clasp, and toss each of our three all-purpose
repellents of all-purpose rain in Earl's Sluice.

They'll sink, each Brolly. Just think how no
more Brolly-weight might feel. We'll let it go,

when the days seem to fall like London snow
not London rain, we'll just let them go.

BRITTEN AND DANTE IN BELFAST

I ran away from home when I was two.
I did not make it very far. What makes you
think I am running now has more to do
with your pantomime of what 'things' two

owe each other. I won't ramble on now
on how Late Capitalism and DOW
indexes mean more to you than what I call
love. Landed now in Belfast, I did call

you as I promised. Call waiting. Tell me: how
many times must we keep waiting? Tattersall
at 16 Skipper, The Merchant, creased by all
I walked not ran away from. That promise. This row.

AIN'T MISBEHAVIN'

This morning I put a dollop of shaving
Cream onto my toothbrush. *Ain't misbehavin'*

Savin' all my love for you. Fats Waller
On the turntable, drowning out missed callers

On the mobile phone I forgot to charge
Last night. I made a modestly large

Cup of tea and poured it on my oatmeal.
God doesn't know where I put the maple

Syrup. Lathering up my shaving brush
In a boxwood bowl of toothpaste now. No rush.

My laundry folded, I'll hoover it, mop
The kitchen counters. When the rain stops,

I'll head out with my brolly neatly furled.
I've got all the time in the world.

JUST SUPPOSING

I'm revisiting room 1514
at the Park Hyatt. That's where I proposed
to you. No tears. Promise. What dry ravine
we forged between us. But now let's suppose

we irrigated the distance in between,
diverted rivers like the Euphrates
in Herodotus' *Histories*.
Suppose that, and suppose also we wean

you off the guilt of dreaming. Do you suppose
this is too much gilding to propose?
Is *not* to deserve something you chose?
Or something one can, and can not, impose?

Tell me. I'm not proposing.
Just supposing.

FAILURE

Let me tell you not what looks like failure
But what failure looks like – the false allure
Of an alleyway which turns out to be true
Reprieve from the intersection where you
Know that one day curve-walking the latitude
Will get you hit (at worst . . . at best, it's rude).
Failure is a basement flat off Dovercourt
Where you court and court and court
The one whose past you alone can reconcile
Save the hostility of the turnstile
Through which you shove with pram and bags and all
To get home, in time, to make that phone call
Which concludes itself in *contrapposto*
With "nite!" and "nite!!" and "XO!!!" – then heart's dull *No*
Which tugs at our Christian-Cartesian split
Of giving up splayed "sparks", giving up on it.

PAS DE DEUX

Having unbuttoned my waistcoat, I find
two expired ballet tickets in the pockets
of my waistcoat. I plug the coffee grind-
er into a too-stiff socket,
the electric kettle into another,
then begin a letter to my brother,
estranged. "Dear Paul . . ." is as far as I get.

I put down my pen
and decide I'll begin
my night by assembling my own life, again.

ROUTE 1

You could spend a lifetime
hoofing the ball up the pitch
to a striker who cannot finish
nor stay onside with runs untimed.

BELFAST LANDING

for E.E.H.

When the plane wobbled in its descent
To George Best Belfast City Airport
I thought of the Munich Air Disaster

Then what came to mind was the descant
I forged between us. Never the sort
To cross myself in polyester

Prayer, I crossed myself and thought of what I meant
When I asked you "Will you marry me?" Short
Of runway, I'm working for our daughter

Whom we don't have yet. These days I rent
A modest basement flat off Dovercourt.
I'm better now, if by better

What is meant is no more descents
No more roller coaster rides to comport
The plane to skid-landing helter-skelter.

SELF-PORTRAIT WITH CITROËN

Up at three thirty-five.
Too late to sleep again, so I drive
Dad's Citroën, 1975
But I don't know how to drive.
But then again, you'd never ever know –
Or would you? The third gear jives just so,
Spastic into fourth, now the heavy clutch is
Sputtering back to me that sound of fizz
Which reeks the whole production
And I suppose my reintroduction
Cannot but be a pithy, apologist
"Hi, mum." I am sorry to say the list
Of things I've got to do has now grown
Longer. I'm fine. Glass ankle stitches sewn.
Back to West Ken – our parking metre's done.
And I am sorry: we are, alas, at one
With the bright "Illegal Parking" ticket
Which isn't true grit. We're missing it.

PHILOCTETES AT THE GYM

No compunction, my physiotherapist
Walks, kale juice in hand, out of The Raw Chemist

With the swagger of a Neoptolemus
Who will lie to me, to you, to all of us

For the sake of winning what he mythifies
As our battle. I watch him pause, flex his thighs,

Take a single, discreet white Pall Mall
(Charcoal filtered) from his Nike carryall.

I tighten the brace back round my ankle
Wondering if and when we're setting sail.

Today the pain in my foot is bearable,
Not so my personnel.

AARON RAMSEY'S VOLLEY AT CARROW ROAD, 11 MAY 2014

Postage stamp, Neronic pirouette,
Ball sent spiralling off the inside post
Centripetally into the net.
After all the troubles, the perfect riposte:

Look your look says looking at no one
In particular. *Look what I just done.*
To all who said you'd never make the grade
After the fracture – here they are, repaid.

ALL THE TIME IN THE WORLD

Now my head is wobbling on the train
from Montreal to Toronto,
my vacant thoughts are tending to go
West by Northeast, wobbling. Now the refrain
of the shuffling carriage-car is a plaintive
horn sounding the rattling, my thoughts give
way to different kinds of arrivals.
A baby's rattle, perhaps, or rivals

made out of siblings who could give a damn
if they were allowed to say the word 'damn'
without the fear of undue repercussion.
Please come collect me at Union Station?
Take your time. Now the track ahead has unfurled
for us, we've got all the time in the world.

HERACLITUS AT THE BASELINE

You, my enemy,
Are not opposite the net
From me. You are me.

SORRY, MUM

To tell you that you sacrificed all sounds trite
but I do wonder, what manner of man might
I be without you? If I'm honest, I'd
still be sailing out of Polzeath at high tide,
just to get your husband's attention.
(NB: That was deliberate, that being
my pointedly not using the word 'father'.)
I'm sorry, Mum, for how many conniption
fits I caused you when my yacht went fleeing
out of Polzeath. If I'm honest, I'd rather
I'd stayed home and made you a very good steak
au poivre. I just didn't know what was at stake
because I was so young and liked life to be
jocular. I took some jokes too far,
like the time I joined The Spiders from Mars.
For any other such worry
as this I ever caused you, Mum, I'm sorry.

OF PURPOSES

for Philip Nikolayev

Peel away the tinsel paper,
The polka-dotted Christmas paper,

The all-purpose paper in the river
Tossed beneath the all-purpose over-

Pass. All-purpose bridges forget what
Passes underneath what 'friends' forgot

Of purposes. Exhausted from homeless
Relocations, I'm buying a townhouse

This afternoon. I saved up for it through
Thirty-five years of roofless. Four floors floor-through

And what's important a ruthful double-door
Egress in Racecar Red. For your office. For

My leaping purposefully upon
The bed of peonies and rhododendron

Planted in the lovely hot pink garden.
I'll somersault, swim my way back to London.

I'm tired of all this relocation.
I'm tired of fake plastic compassion.

I want real compassion or no compassion
At all. Having reaped what I have sown

I shall land softly on the rhododendron
And backstroke my way back home to London.

SPY VS. SPY

Up I grew as down you went a foxhole.
I used to think you were a proper spy,
three-piece chalk-striped chauffeured, surreptitious eye
storing everything: this freckle, that mole,
nothing escaped your surreptitious eye.
Except me. Somehow I raced through on goal –
unmarked – and then smashed a gaping hole
in the onion bag. What misery
all down Seven Sisters! Highbury
had never seen such joy since the Thierry
Henry era! I barged into your bedroom
one night with a hollowed-out turnip on a stick.
You paid no attention at first. You just slicked
back your jet-black-dyed hair with crème silk groom
and shot me a bloodshot look. I didn't ask
you nor tell mum about your capsized flask.
Before I sent this out, I caught an error
in verse 6 above. I wrote "Accept me"
whilst clearly what was meant was "Except me".
My first lecture on Ovid stressed how *error*
and *crimen* were two quite separate concepts
in Augustan Rome, how banished voices kept
less sane in relegation than in exile.
He had to leave it all behind, with style
if not grace, and suffer the anxious knowing
that he might, just might, some sweet day, be recalled
to Rome. I thought of Ovid when I called
to tell you I was coming home. My growing
up as down you went, down another foxhole . . .
all these years later I still think of exile,
relegation, and I'm still not quite sure

which one of the two I should prefer –
when I think of how up I grew I smile
because my smile's one thing I can sometimes find
in Polaroid 100 Sepia style
albums in the atelier. The *via*
media is where I'm content, where I grind
out a poem or review or article,
faithful, diplomatic, ruthlessly loyal –
except for calling your bluff and outing
you, ousting you, with the Consul General:
I could've done with being poor; but spouting
lies, that was your trade, and now you're pouting
over the makeshift deathbed whose hospital-
corners you made yourself and remade
with a protractor. Here you lie, repaid.
So I'll stay on the *via media*, grind
out another poem, live on the dole and smile
and try to be happy, though bad as a mile
and a country mile behind.

THESE PREMISES ARE ALARMED

Just about this time last year I met
a fabulous confabulator –
don't think this is aposiopesis
nor fabulist on my part: just let
me, please, tell you the truth about her:
just allow me this raw and pithy list
of lies she spun and even had tattooed
all over her skin like so many skeins
of needle-inked-in 'art' recounting pains
she said she had endured. For months I, too,
endured those confabulations as though true.
For starters, she was from Kalamazoo,
or I should say '*is* from', because last
I checked, she's still alive – if not quite with us.
I wouldn't call her a con artist
but she is (or was) as close to one as I
have ever met. She's from Kalamazoo
and every word above and below is true.
On her left hip, if ever you set eye
there, the first thing you will notice is a blue
spider. It is from her first failed marriage.
Was there more than one? Well, I won't blame my age,
which was half her age then, but I believed her
when she told me, "I just, like, *love* the colour
blue! And I happen to think the spider
is a fascinating animal." Never
had I thought of spiders as animals,
though of course the spider is an animal –
if I'm honest, an anthropogenic
fault of my own, that. But back to brass-tacks.
The blue spider tattooed on her left hip

turned out to be not just some inked-in hip-
sterism but the 'Something Blue' – she swore –
something borrowed, and also new, she wore
on her (first?) wedding day: she said she'd forgot
that 'Something Blue' but her friend, a Goth
(in today's unfaithful sense, it must be stressed)
was dressed as Goths, I suppose, do dress: distressed,
in a word. This form of distress the Goth-friend
lent was a blue ring in the shape of a blue
spider bought at Mile End, or World's End, – "*Ayng*land",
with a twang, the girl from Kalamazoo
(not the Goth but the fatal fabulist)
was wont to say in what seemed deceptive
intonations then – though now I chalk this
up to her plain, home-on-the-range ignorance.
You must believe me, this isn't invective:
I'm only trying to convey a sense
of the confabulator without what sounds
like what so many fabulists I found
in my previous life in Kalamazoo
might design. Now to return to the tattoos.
She rhapsodised them as being 'epic'.
I didn't tell her that they made me sick,
that an epic is a type of poem,
that you can't just call something worth writing home
about 'epic' just because it's hip. She had
that hipster flair for coopting things past –
archaeologist hopped up on AutoCAD
trying to pass off a sort of anti-past
of vinyl dubbed off USB. It won't last.
I'm so, so tired of Kalamazoo,
a town I just happened to be passing through
on a desultory trip through Michigan
on my way from Chicago to where I am

now, shaving my face in Toronto,
still reeling in shame from the scam
that almost reeled me in. Wherever I go
now and meet someone new, my first question is:
"Do you have a tattoo?" I ask this,
because I once knew a fabulist
from Kalamazoo . . . Aposiopesis
kicks in. Off of it, I'm off to make breakfast.

TRIDENTINE MASS FOR HARD TIMES

i.m. R. S. Thomas 1913-2000

Awake at 5am on a Sunday
we must be Bacchic dipsomaniacs
or Tiresian insomniacs . . .
Boy, boy: I'm tired from talking: take me away

from here and leave this man to rage at himself . . .
But we're on our way to High Mass, a mass
for hard times, for when I look at our bookshelves
I see books double-backed like bus routes amassed

over the years as replacement copies
for the ones I sold in leaner years than these.
"There were such things" – I'll sit you on my knees
one day and say – "as years where salaries

were frozen, you'd take your severance and walk
away with some semblance of dignity
but not much else." Our son (it's a boy, yes?) balks
at my impecunious fantasy –

my *Chanson de la folle au bord de la mer*
(for of course our son is steeped in Charles-
Valentin Alkan and learned the clavier
before he could say *papa* or even crawl) –

much like me confused why we had a driver
who drove us round from embassies to bistro-
bar-cafés yet I had to use a Biro
Minor while Ollie had a Montclair

fountain pen and a Yard-O-Led pencil
both stamped approvingly with his initials.
Awake at 5am on a Sunday –
these, my darling, are such thoughts as chip away

at my impinged right shoulder that has no chips
on it, no sharp things to grind, just this old Krups
grinder for the coffee beans for I'm always
awake at 5am on a Sunday,

knotting my Grove House tie for High Mass,
always a rectangular knot, dimple
always ending the groove asymmetrical . . .
I used to think Tridentine Mass

had to do with Neptune, or Tiresias
with distaff – I, Anglican but born Sikh,
who never sat on dad's knees to hear him speak
about lean years, High Mass, how hard times amass.

WHEN WILL HIS STUPID HEAD REMEMBER?

It was a *dignified* way to go,
your retirement – Regency style, two sharp
jabs, I'm told, through a double-glazed window,
in your Savile Row suit, lapels so sharp

ending in corners that could cut as deep
as the glass that cut your fists, or the blasts
of vitriol and spittle because I keep
my bankbook as scratched-up as the calfskin last-

made shoes I chucked in the dustbin at long last –
your 'gift' swapped for . . . my own crêpe-soled chukka boots!
They chafe my heels sometimes when I sprint past
buses to show how fast I am. The abuse

of unlined suede on sockless skin, I prefer
that to blasts of vitriol and spittle.
The shoestrings do break sometimes: they're brittle
from so much running past now, now after

buses. The insole's impressed by my footprint
so deep that my toes can squirm through the rubber
crêpe sole. WHEN WILL HIS STUPID HEAD REMEMBER?
It doesn't have to remember. It's in print,

it's in poems you've never read and never will,
it's in my PhD thesis, my first book,
the chapter on Antigone and free will . . .
"The Creons of the world are those who shook

Thebes; neither the Tyrant's son's will nor God's will . . . "
It's also written all over my face. Look.
But you never will
because it's not a bill.

MUSKOKA

I lay awake awaiting my mobile's
ringing a ring which pantomimes "old phone"
among the "folder" of audio "files"
dubbed "Classic". I change the dial tone
to "Mamba". Perhaps I got the style
all wrong. Perhaps nearby I'll find slim stones
and skip them clear a country mile
away. Texts. Emails. No one ever phones.

ESCARPMENT

We're each of us too clever to believe
in such a thing as The One. Maple leaves
on Norway maple trees outside your window
are now red at best . . . at worst the wind blows
them into the escarpment. Where'd it go,
Summer? Right *robbed* us. Broad daylight. I know.

HIGHBURY HAIKU

I
A sliver of mauve
Sky skims over Holloway.
Silverware, they crave.

II
Purple rain, purple
Rain, purple hoops round the Grove.
Highbury is flats.

III
Resite the Clock End,
Resite, too, Ferrier's bust.
Leave Lough Road a waste.

IV
Monday's child, Arsène
Out; Tuesday's, Arsène knows best.
Garrotte him again.

V
Spiegel im Spiegel.
Jeers ring round the Allianz.
Substitute Özil.

VI
Giroud flicks the ball
On, a cute little back-heel,
Ineffectual.

VII
Transfer window closed.
I noticed lots of strikers.
Could use one of those.

VIII
Diaby's got flu.
The match-day programme says so
So it must be true.

IX
Remember Steve Bould,
Adams, Dixon, Winterburn!
Now Bould marks zonal.

X
Mannone, man on
The far post – Mannone, out
To lunch, out on loan.

XI
Bendtner's lost his sense.
Had he sense to begin with
Why the Paddy pants?

LEAVING MONTRÉAL

The *côtelette d'agneau*
Traipses onto my tongue so
So much "I love you".

I TOOK A TRIP ON A TRAIN

I took a trip on a train from Gargrave
to Longhope through Badwell Ash and Modney
for no real reason other than it gave
me respite to relight the dimming memory
that we used to take a trip on a train
for the sake of taking a trip on a train.

I took a trip on a train from Gargrave
and I did not think about you until
I passed a single smokestack among windmills
and the windmills' churning industry forgave
the smokestack's inefficient exhalations
as though to breathe alone it shuns

so many years of science passed between
its cloud morphed slow into a protean
zoo of carbon monoxide animals . . .
well, that's when I thought about you, banal
though it might seem – what a difference it makes,
patient turbines there; here, smoke-hazed fist-shakes
obsoletely energetic, canals
of shapes of things which, out of thick air, I fake.

THE REBEL HOUSE

We get off at the wrong stop, bicycle
what must be the length of a difficult book
uphill. You're complaining that The Rebel

House is like *so* not on the way. On the way
to where, I wonder. You look a look
like it's my fault now your trouser hems are frayed.

SCENERY

Scenery. My Bibiji learns
A new word. Staring at the snow
Confection on the ferns
She says *scenery.* I say *I know.*

SOME SWEET DAY

She bawled *You pathological* this-and-that . . .
Thanks, I said. I'll get that looked at.
I rolled my umbrella, took my coat and hat,
And walked away to where our age is what we act.

SUNCHOKES

are not artichokes at all but tubers.
At the neurologist's you squeeze my hand
Too hard for my liking. We won't say tumour
At all. They've called it a growth. The rubber band

Retreats, acrobats in baby blue disband,
Sighing. I'm beside myself with fleeting thoughts
Of fleeing; you're beside me with your garrotte
Of choked-back tears, handcuffing my hand.

TABULA RASA NUMQUAM

I'm glad we didn't buy that orchid last
Saturday; glad, too, that we came home past
two AM, so the bars were closed; glad we passed
that Bosnian café: it had just lost,
I'm glad, its liquor license. Glad the cost
(beyond my lawyer's not unduly modest
retainer fee) is joblessness at best,
at worst, deportation from this somewhere
where I have no longer any interest.
That juried orchid show, I'll remember us there,

while here, at the airport, blurred photographs
in faux-sepia scroll past me on my
binge-razed tablet. To add captions I must buy
the app. No thanks. No more epitaphs.

LORD'S

"If I were captain, I'd settle for nowhere
else but silly point." Nothing was sillier
to you than the *Wisden Cricketers'*

Almanack. The Ashes – we sat in the sun.
Hatless, you loathed the whole pavilion
and walked away till your laces came undone.

THE SIGHT OF A GOOSE GOING BAREFOOT

Satisfied by the enormous condescension
of posterity and the iron
logic of predestination,
you could blot out time, could make abjection be
but poles of covetousness: they repel me.
But the time of abjection is double,
now oblivion and veiled infinity,
now chock-a-block with toe-curling sentiment,
flotsam and jetsam of rail-
way stations. It will all end in tears:
me, brisk, bracing, and irreverent;
you, goose gone barefoot on the *via
media*, martyr's grin worn ear to ear,
grieving the loss of your mania.

CRINOIDS

Saying goodnight on her gravel driveway
north of Coventry, she stops and stoops
to show me rocks – little ridged sand-coloured tubes
which, in prehistoric seas, she says,
were flowers with six-foot stalks and lily-sprays
of stems on top so that these now-fossils look
threaded, like so many mangled screws.
Sometimes, she says, if you find them *in situ*,
you can make out longer stretches and – look!
she says – trace the branch between the stalk
and what was once a flower. I balk:
surely, not a word of this is true.
Sifting gravel, I find none. She finds two
and she says "they're for you."

I saved them, fossils found in limestone laid
down over ancient seas, she said,
and because that limestone is quarried
for gravel, the fossils show up in Coventry driveways.
I keep the rocks she gave me buried
in the breast pocket of the blazer I wore
that night. Sixteen, unsure how long I'd stay
in England, desperate to avoid
the thought of more
relocations, I turn those rocks – crinoids,
she said – between my fingers. Just rocks,
which somewhere, some time, were flower-stalks.

ETC.

for L.E.M.

We rowed out to Paquachuck Inn
Too late to get the morning papers.
All week we had been sleeping in;
All night we'd listen to the breakers'
Slow consoling roar
After days spent on the shore
In rippling arguments
Among the salty scents
Of Buzzard's Bay.
I won't forget that one calm day
We rowed out to the Inn at last in time
To get the papers: that air of kelp and thyme
And you stay with me in East Anglia,
Anglesey, Polzeath, Daymer . . . etc.

KEMPLAY ROAD

When I left the Kemplay Road this afternoon
the morning's mist was turning into raindrops.
I waited underneath the awning
for a taxi which did not arrive as soon
as promised. I watched two girls in flip-flops
hurry to their car beneath a yawning
inside-out umbrella; they laughed loudly
as they flip-flopped. Brave peonies opened
on this first of June – bloody fools, their cloudy
petals plucked out by the wind.

I wanted to go home.
But when the taxi got to Paddington
I thought of you alone in Rome
and missed both trains in hesitation.

MANCHESTER DAYDREAM
ON THE JUBILEE LINE

for M.E.B.

Dimly I remember, when I turn dim lights
of goddamned memory lower, daydream kites
and your corduroy on a makeshift football
pitch in front of Hamilton Hall. What a ball
we had. Your artless smile, pinwale, tattersall,
mismatched mauve: you recede like city lights
in the rear-view to Morningside Heights . . .
Dimmer still I recall *verum velle*
parum est, an A62 melee,
ostentatious London Pride and cigarettes,
Wearside wishes, presupposed regrets.

Now please describe the city lights once more,
mismatch again your mauve and tattersall
before I remember to forget it all
when I recede again to Polzeath shore.
Surely life can live outside our Grappenhall?
Awake now. Jubilee Line. Stanmore.
Sorry. Wrong line. Missed the Heath. Missed your call.

WHAT THE WIND DOES TO THE RAIN

Reflected in the windowpane
of the rattling train
your face starts to ripple in the starting rain
but then the lights go out again
and flicker with the jolting train.
When the lights come back again
I watch the slant-wise wind-swept London rain
wash your face from the window pane.
Then my love looks all in vain,
I look beyond your face in vain,
and all that's left is the dull pain
of pushing you away again
the way sometimes it's not so much the rain
as what the wind does to the rain.

PANIC

Side A: *Introit*

He stumbled through the door and smashed the frame
of the painting hanging to his left right
before he fell prostrate in the half-light
lit enough to let her know things were the same
but for the fact that this time it was his right
knee not his left that was left bruised in the fall.
Next week he stumbled through the door to call
an ambulance because he thought he was
having a heart-attack, but first he found
the time to kick to bits her flower vase
on the bookcase until the sound
awoke her: still he contrived to know the frame
of mind in which she was: "he weeps in shame;
the lies change; still he stays the same…".

Side B: *Exeunt omnes*

He stumbled through the door and smashed the frame
of the door with the one crutch he used to use
for his broken right leg because he left
the other crutch at the pub the name
of which he can't recall for he'd choose
a different pub each night for he was deft
enough so as to leave no trail of credit-
card receipts which she might see. Fuck it:
the painting to the right side of the door
is in the dustbin, proof that he had more,
from a bottle he hid behind the bookcase
just in case she might decide "No more"
and take one look at his lying face
and walk out of the door.

THE ROT, *OR* SUICIDE ON CURZON STREET, MAYFAIR, 1828

The rot that seeped off of his badger-bristle
stag-horn shave brush made him think the kill
still lived. After every shave it left a stain
of brown-green round the basin
and pink soap splashes on the shaving mirror.
Three times each morning he would lather
up his face to shave: with the grain, against it,
and a third time just to taste the rose scent
on his lips. It used to be his wife had stood
behind him, holding to her nose the boxwood
bowl of perfumed soap, but also rot
that seeped off of the stag-horn. He forgot
himself, often cut himself, then insisted
"I have changed". She left. The rot persisted.

AVE MARIA

Each evensong he woke and cued
the gramophone to Schubert's
Ave Maria. He would brood
over the sharpness of his Spartacus
buffalo-horn-handle razor
before the shaving mirror
then glide the razor cross his face.
True, it was a facile piece,
but the way Ossy Renardy
played it had the plain solemnity
of music strained at by a child
for whom fidelity to score is style.
Most mornings by the fourth repeat he'd rinse
his face, but Christmas last he slit his wrists.

CHILDS HILL

Six months later out of the womb for eight
hours and you're gone. I'm sorry I was late
at Gatwick but I couldn't hit eject
(our Starman days, they're gone, correct?)
and stop the jet's petrol-blasting taxi
nor advance in the queue for a taxi
with sincere words – "Please, my nephew is dead".
They don't believe me: after all, they've just read
in flight about who fucked who and whether
Rooney's bicycle kick came off his shin
or "He done laced it!" This isn't London
any more but a mobile with a tether
to every other sputtering machine . . .
The casket was painfully light at Golders Green.

FOOLS LIKE ME

Am I not ridiculous,
listening to the susurrus
of wind among my Norway maple's leaves
and fancying it grieves
the end of us.

For only fools like me believe
that when the loved one leaves
her ghost will always haunt the purlieus
of his silent house
like timid thieves.

WHAT DAMN GOOD

I stored your picture in a box
with your farewell letter, pants, and socks.
"Yours sincerely" is our epitaph.
When your last word, as final as Scripture,
is worth a thousand pictures,
what damn good's a photograph.

RAILWAY STATIONS

After lunch in Marylebone,
I tried to find a telephone
To ring you up before
My train at four

To Oxford. But I was running late,
And knowing it was only eight
AM for you, I fetched
A black cab, watching London stretched

Out in the sun,
Rushing past me – Kensington,
Then Knightsbridge slipped away
Against the noonday

Failing light. The train pulled out
From Paddington with shouts
Of "Slough!" resounding
In the railcar. "Reading!"

Jolted me awake:
The grinding of the brakes
Filled me with the sense of consolation
I've always felt in railway stations.

But after a minute or two,
My thoughts lurched back to you:
Different landscapes; different names;
My loneliness remains the same.

HERRINGBONE

This morning breakers off of Polzeath shore
aren't breaking as they broke before
those hours which we spent ashore alone
and watched the rippled herringbone
the dinghies left behind them
as they went away the way the trouser-hem
of ocean goes away from Polzeath shore
then brings the dinghies back ashore:

the way that I can rest assured
that you will go away once more
and leave me on the shore alone
but come back in an inverse herringbone
so neat and arrowed and intent
as Ocean's made-to-measure argument.

FALL IS SO SAD

Fall is so sad. Last night's chilling rain
Has taken down the golden leaves
And pasted them against my window-pane.
Now my Norway maple tree's
Left bare, trembling as it were in pain.

The remnant leaves, so many outstretched hands,
Reach westward for the Hudson River.
This is their final dance,
The dying days of late November,
The season's closing sarabandes.

DERBY DAY

We seat ourselves at the Polish café
and order the same omelette. Derby Day,
Merseyside; Derby Day, North London.
Jagielka, in extra time added on,
clean volleys it, thirty clean yards out,
smashes the postage stamp with such doubt
that the mail will come back, like my MRI,
postage due, ball spiralling like you and I.

MILTON IN AORIST

I'll take the number 30 bus to Kipling.
The GO train to Milton. I do these things
to keep me in suspense. Staring out rear
windows, mind and chequebook in arrears.

YOUR TUMBLER

You lift your tumbler too ice-full and thump
the tumbler on the burl wood bar, audibly.
It could be her. It could be me.
It could be your shoulders slumped
just so: not drunk but 'tipsy'
as if there's a difference between three
and nine when you've lost count of what you were count-
ing on counting on in the first place.
Suddenly, the barmaid has a face
of porcelain. Suddenly, you're a Viscount.

NO VACANCY

The sutures. As the surgeon unstitches
Them I'm full of vacant thoughts of stitching
My life back again. But the hitches
Along the way . . . how back to pitching
Stories to the BBC after such
A long hiatus. How it takes so much
To reassemble legs and lives, so little
For all the lives we live to unravel.

JUKEBOXES

We played our youths out on jukeboxes
And danced until we had to darn our socks.
We squandered so much money
On so many jukeboxes . . . Sugar Pie Honey
Bunch, that was your "most favourite in the world".
Our shoelaces came undone, our curls uncurled,
We played our youths out on jukeboxes
Until your bouts of pancreatitis
Taught us to leave our youths behind us.

SHAKESPEARE AT THE BASELINE

The net's a hard pinch.
Necessity does pinch hard.
Hawk. Eye. I. Chalk. Inch.

DANTE AT THE BASELINE

I wear seven P's
On my brow. Advantage out.
Let. No applause please.

THE SPIDERS FROM MARS, ENCORE

I joined The Spiders from Mars in nineteen-
Eighty-six. I left them when I turned eighteen
And was old enough to buy my own gin,
My very own Crystal Palace Gin. The grin
I wore with my Jack Purcells rang in the Blur
Era. I knew when my mother and father
Could be heard saying goodnight to their chauffeur,
I'd eighty-six seconds to rehearse my "Sir"
In the right Harrovian intonation,
Hide the packet of Dunhills, and the gin,
And be present in the foyer, no grin,
Just pomaded, black-tied, boatered mannequin.

CANTONA

Every football fan saw this in Ninety-six:
Your use of McClair to circumvent
An entire midfield. The boot's caress,
Insouciant, of the ball. The flat movement
Of said ball arcs a wearied Wearside defence.
Collar turned-up. Stationary. Fat. Dense
Monobrow. Not one jot of penitence.
The Platonic Ideal of Impudence.

TIC-TAC-TOE

I never did ask
You to meet my xox
With another x.

One o after x
Can be enough of a task
In a mid-day text.

QUITE A SCARE

How did you end up in my nightmare?
I gave you and you gave me quite a scare.
Did you know I had a nightmare?
Did you now? Did you know I was down there
Clinging to your ribcage beneath the covers
Before I came up for air?
You might have known, because you
Sighed and ran your fingers through
My steel-wool hair
Confirming, so nice and politely, you're here.
In my dream I slid down the bannister
So fast I broke not only my femur
But also yours, a triple-compound fracture
If that exists. It doesn't, says the doctor.

SHIMALA

After weeks of humid weather
rain at last arrived with thunder's leather
thwack. I listen to the tapping plant box,
tin and water, wondering where the downpour
caught you. Prospect Park? The drugstore?
A night without torrential 'talks'.

Shirtless with a *rakhri* on my right wrist
I'm reminded of Manali's monsoon mist
one August after eating *dhal* and *saag*
at a roadside *dhabha*. I recall
the countless outsize moths dying in the hall
of our 'hotel' like a mono, crackling raga.

The first time back I was five.
I managed to stay alive
by drinking Coca-Cola (Made in Delhi)
and gnawing on the stalks of sugarcane
upon our riverbanks. Months of bug-bite pain,
crying to go home, an aching belly.

I awake to find despite the smell
of dirt and rain I'm in New York, well
into a sultry summer, listening
to the raindrops turn to drizzle which falls
in arpeggios. No one calls.
I watch the pavement glistening.

After an hour's wait I lock
the door, and although waiting for that knock,
at last turn off the lights and lay above

the covers. I must remember
not to lose my temper.
I must remember how to love.

RAINFALL, SLIGO

October rain that's fallen now
For four days in a row
Does not look like abating now
But falling for a fifth day in a row
And making now a five-day fog lie low
And glide like the cigarette smoke I blow
Lying this morning against my pillow
Where rainfall helps me fall asleep again now
Chain-smoking and smoke-enchained in Sligo.

PROVIDENCE, PROVIDENCE

As we wound our eastward way to Westport
Point, leaving New York behind us,
the sunlit snow began to blind us.
Children now tobogganed, now built forts,
now threw snowballs at our train
whose horn kept bellowing and waking us
who knew, and didn't, where it was taking us.
And then the conductor's insistent refrain,

as still reeds rose from the water banks,
as still as the distant water-tanks,
Providence, Providence, Providence . . .
as your sighs grew more drawn-out and vexed,
as my eyes were lulled by the snowfall-dance,
Providence, Providence, Providence is next . . .

A COUNTRY MILE BEHIND

You drank too much last night at Picholine
And woke this morning with the dull impression
That by our dinner's end our talk turned mean.
Damn these old regressions
Which end our evenings out
With someone cursing someone out
Once 'things' of the heart get out.
Though I always hope the good will out,
In future I will keep the bad tucked in,
Neat as a napkin
Tucked into my waistcoat for your smile.
I'm sorry that you rose today to find
My heart's bad as a mile
And a country mile behind.

DACRYOSTENOSIS

"Did I tell you I was born without tear ducts?"
she begins. No, you didn't. She corrects
herself: "I mean I was born with my tear ducts

closed, and the doctor asked my mama if she
wanted them opened." These canaliculi
lacrimae, they open up now audibly

late at night tears that retreat down the phone cord
and every time her tears fall I think, *Lord,*
thank you that her tired tears aren't stored

away, thank you that such information
as she only sheds at night isn't hidden
away from me. Keep falling. I'll listen.

CLINK OF ICE

The opal pendant necklace, frail
As your hamstring you pulled playing baseball,

Draped your neck but for five, maybe six, hours.
This birthday gift was yours, is yours,

But the melee (let's face it) was ours.
Mine mostly but I won't cower

Underneath your super-capacity
To hate. Giving you of your semblances of me

Wears me out. I'd keep my chin higher if
This parting were down to me, each tiff

Down to my disused spectacles.
The waiter takes our order, refills

The water in our carafe.
You're having a laugh

If you reckon each clink of ice cubes
Didn't make me think of you

And what electric coldness can contrive.
Thank God, or curse God, that we're still alive.

HOME

How you fumble back upstairs with your
Yoga mat and bicycle, soaked to the skin.
How you sob "I won't do this again".
How you still don't know how to lock the door.

LEG BEFORE WICKET

I walked you to your tube stop
Listening to the clip-clop, clip-clop
Of your ill-fitting 'pumps' the whole way.
It can't always be this way,
Can it? Waiting for the telephone
Not to ring with another way
Out of meeting again, at Future Café,
Where you eat half my scone
With an aspartamed latte
And leave alone. Which is to say
Together we part each night anyway.
But there is this thing we call tomorrow.
I'll meet you there with *Hatful of Hollow*.

FEDERER

The insouciance of the backhand,
hilt of racket
drawn from the pocket;
the reprimand
from the crowd, unduly loud,
due to one whispered expletive.
We live what lives we live
and forget
how close we could, just could,
arrive at the net
and unsimply tap the ball,
not noticing gravity at all.

THERE, THERE

You broke the habit of a lifetime when
You said sorry for walking out again.
The London sky, mauve and indecisive;
Me looking for a pub, you for Big Ben:
The chimes were not unduly incisive
As you fumbled, fought, through the *A to Z*
To find some sort of route from Berkeley Square
To what you'd mapped out: there, and there, and *there* . . .
There, there, my darling – I'll soon be in bed
And, dreaming, see through everything you do.
I see through everything you do.
I rest my head upon our weary bed
And warily count the sheep of dues:
The electric bill, three book reviews . . .
What to say to you? I've no clue.

EDGBASTON

Do you know the malaise of walking
To the wicket? One fan flips a V-sign,
Another bitches about the umpire;
A neophyte not even watching
Derides sledging as metaphor for empire.
My captain tells me, "Just smash it, son" –
So I shall, and have done. Have done.
I am the nightwatchman of Edgbaston.

BUT THE RATTLE

He bowled a bouncer. I recall
but the rattle of the cricket ball
in my helmet, then unorigined calls
of 'medic!' echoing round Edgbaston.
When I woke up, my nose was Roman,
my left eye squinting like a hustler's – beady,
chalking-up some cue with feigned indignity.

NORTH EAST EXPRESS

Reckoning an easy ingress and egress
We take the North East Express
To New Delhi – thirty-three
Fast hours from Guhawati.
Tobaccoed windows frame reprieve,
Shin-pads in my football kit some greaves
Against a tackle, cleats up, on my shin.
Trite: of course I take it on the chin.
You turn your laptop away from my sight.
I lose vision of your fiscal site,
Your settling the end of a marriage
In this jolting sleeping carriage.
When we arrive at our hotel
Please, please, please, just don't let loose all hell.

RING

I search her hands for the sight of a ring.
There's none in its proper site. Rain, please bring
Some sleep tonight, some salve against the sight
Of the staunch back of her bicycling
North away from me into the South Ken night.

SPACE

Having laboured over a letter
in the old epistolary sense
I edit the tense –
inceptive imperfect – which got the better
of me when I thought 'things' were going
and going upwards and onwards. No knowing
of barometric pressure. We were going . . .
going . . . going . . . then gone –
you're headed on the northbound 41
somewhere, North. I suppose I'll always be one
to chase buses, late as the phone call
sending sympathies, late as curtain-calls
on the play I really was writing
(and even starred in) whilst we were fighting
over this thing you spaciously call 'space':
if you need it, tell me: what and where's this place?

NO ALARMS

How many times must I awake to Tango
Or some such simulacrum of "Time to go
To work"? We tried Mamba, Stars, even Silhouette.
But no quiddity of beeps can get
Me out of bed when I curl sideways to find
You're not beside me and I am weeks behind.

SELF-PORTRAIT WITH COMPOSURE

For god's sake, how many hours have gone by
since she said she'd call to say she's landed
safely in New York? Perhaps she's stranded
at the airport in Toronto and my
inability to drive a car
is to blame, is blameworthy, is blamed. Far
away from a pensive stroll in the alley-
way behind my Junction basement flat
she's likely to have uncorked some cheap Chablis
or some *méthode champenoise* for it is that
time of day when you indulge whilst I carve
my face with tea and worry. This knife. That scarf.

AMALGAMEMNONS

You bought weak tea, I a cup (whose stench,
at least, was one) of coffee in Regent's Park.
You were disappointed when we found a bench
at last where I could elevate
my splinted leg. We'll sit here till it's dark
enough to go home, home to our separate
homes. You chastised me for recycling
my coffee cup: "It doesn't go in *that* bin.
It's not recyclable." Unlearn a new thing
everyday. Now all those bobby pins
you've littered round my flat . . . my eye for vengeance
sees their recyclable reticulations
soiling my dustbin. Amalgamemnons –
how these two rights will contrive to make a wrong.

THE NINETIES

for Richard Brammer

If I'm honest about the nineties, all
I remember are those over-the-ball
Tackles by Cantona, Liam pleading
"Stand by me", pappardelle kneading
All the rage, and this is the next century
With iron lungs and is it really
Really really really gonna happen.
I remember now's supposed to be then
When Jarvis Cocker wished to see you there
Standing only in your underwear.

THESE ARE DAYS

He scolds me for wearing a corduroy
jacket in sub-minus weather. Berkeley,
I blame. Another scolds me that the soy-
beans in my salad lack vitamin D.
These are my salad days. These are days
which I devote to polishing my boots
and replacing each and every lace.
These are days I'm skint, eating bamboo shoots.

LEICESTER CITY

Drinkwater slips the ball through to Mahrez
And an entire bank of an offside trap
Collapses. Vardy earns another cap
For England, the BBC pundit says.
Finding Vardy, Leicester City pauses,
Running down ostensibly lost causes.

MY BIRTHDAY PRESENTS

On a Roncesvalles rapprochement we stopped
at Cookery: The Art of Cooking. Hopped-

up on caffeine, over-steeped Earl Greyer,
hopped-up on a glimmer of a prayer

of a glimpse of making everything
right again – you had even worn your ring –

I gazed at Le Creuset's *mini cocotte*:
red, enamelled, and mercifully not

made in Thailand like their heavy-gauge steel
stockpots. Admiring the *cocottes* I steel

myself against the thought that I'll cook two
cottage pies for us, eat both without you.

I wonder, as you drive home to Milton
in tears, why you bought me two instead of one.

SELF-PORTRAIT WITH ORTHOGRAPHY

As I relearn the Gurmukhi alphabet
One of the letters I learn I've forgot
Is the first letter of my surname:
Dhadhaa, with onkar subscript: a frame
Of obstinate cantilevers,
Directionlessly horizontal,
With a "U" floating in between, never
Looking like noticing gravity at all.

AGED TWELVE YEARS

"I'd like to have a word with you," begins
my father. How many words, I wonder,
how many man-hours will be squandered
and tossed into the overflowing dustbin
of boredom inflicted on my schoolboy
holidays? "You're too old to play with toys."
I want to say that poetry is not mere play –
but instead contrive to ruin the holidays.

Before the Prefect of Police for Uttar
Pradesh arrives for dinner, I find my Cutty
Sark Scots Whisky – Aged Twelve Years – neatly stowed
away in a hatbox beneath my boater
in a duffle bag beneath my guest-bed.
"I'm *filthy* from playtime . . . bath-time now," I goad
my father. There was nothing to be said
when I slept through dinner in an empty
bathtub, bestirring myself but once to pee.

SOMETHING TO WRITE HOME ABOUT

for Hannah

I didn't break the saw-blade when cutting silver
in your studio. I see a mauve sliver

of cloud in the pearl. We're sleeping earlier,
you and I. Earlier today, my father

removed his reading glasses: "After two years
in Toronto, you have nothing to show for

your life." I stared at his tie, the mauve sliver
of the groove meeting the dimpled half-Windsor.

Well, what *have* I done? Ended a palaver
which is something to write home about after

I didn't break the saw-blade when cutting silver
in your studio. I see a mauve sliver

of cloud in the peering pearl of sun over
parks where I broke my nose on the Big Dipper.

I didn't break the saw-blade when I cut silver
in your studio. I woke up in Dover

aghast at what order jewellery
can make from disjointedness. Like you, like me.

DRY CLEANERS

This is the time of day to pout and putter,
Pout and putter round about the garden.
Now is the time of day to shout and flutter,
Shout and flutter round about what happened.
Tonight will be the time to scout and mutter,
To capsize and suss out sofa cushions
For the loose change of "You're forgiven",
Change so loose it can never get lost again.
At long last this is the time of day
You sit still. You watch the Norway maples sway.
Now's when you reckon years have not been leaner.
Now's when, suit buttons cracked, you curse dry cleaners.
Like Father Brown, you count the collect,
And search for something resembling a cigarette.

DEUTERONOMY

Slowly now snow in the windowpane
Of the quarry-faced ashlar melts. Baroque.
Quick now creeps in dislocation's pain:
Right shoulder. Cortisone shot. Shock.
Sleet resounds on the gable cornice.
Upgraded to subluxation, I leave
The hospital in tears. The well-worn sleeve
Of the right arm of the midnight blue three-piece
Suit delivers comfort that all in this
What we call living wants darning, is frayed.
Recall now wild roses tea-cupped, displayed
On the bar trolley. Recall now nights spent
On the North East Express. Durham, I will
Be back soon. Some sweet day, with centre vent
Splayed against all wind and snow and fashion;
Deuteronomy and love will spill
On every pew. Incongruous?
Well. What about us. What about us.

ACKNOWLEDGMENTS

I would like to thank the editors of the following
publications, in which some of the poems in this book
first appeared:

Arion: 'An Achaean Suitor'; *The Common*: 'But the
Rattle', 'Dacryostenosis', 'Philoctetes at the Gym'; *The
Hudson Review*: 'Railway Stations'; *The New Criterion*:
'Etc.'; *The Ocean State Review*: 'Butler Library';
'Providence, Providence'; *Parnassus*: 'Nothing To Be
Done'; *PN Review*: 'Sunchokes', 'I Took a Trip on a
Train', 'The Sight of a Goose Going Barefoot'.

EYEWEAR PUBLISHING